# The prevention of violence in sport

**Manuel Comeron**
**Hooliganism Prevention**
**City of Liège (Belgium)**

Integrated project "Responses to violence in everyday life in a democratic society"

Council of Europe Publishing

French edition:

*La prévention de la violence dans le sport*

ISBN 92-871-5037-0

*This text was commissioned by the Sport Department of the Directorate of Youth and Sport of the Council of Europe. The opinions expressed in this work are those of the author(s) and do not all necessarily reflect the official policy of the Council of Europe.*

*All rights reserved. No part of this publication may be reproduced or transmitted in any form or by any means, electronic (CD-Rom, Internet, etc.) or mechanical, including photocopying, recording or any information storage or retrieval system, without the prior permission in writing from the Publishing Division, Communication and Research Directorate.*

Cover design: Graphic Design Workshop, Council of Europe

Council of Europe Publishing
F-67075 Strasbourg Cedex

ISBN 92-871-5038-9
© Council of Europe, December 2002
Printed at the Council of Europe

## INTEGRATED PROJECT "RESPONSES TO VIOLENCE IN EVERYDAY LIFE IN A DEMOCRATIC SOCIETY"

There is an acute awareness and concern about violence and its effects on individuals and society as a whole throughout Europe. Individual security is threatened in everyday life in a wide array of circumstances and places: at home, school, work, sports events and in streets. While violence and fear of violence affects the quality of life of the entire population, certain groups of people may be perceived as specific targets of violence, such as women, children and older persons as well as migrants, refugees and ethnic groups.

The integrated project "Responses to violence in everyday life in a democratic society" has been set up by the Secretary General of the Council of Europe to address these widely shared concerns by mobilising the resources of the organisation for a three-year period, 2002/04. The primary objective of the project is to help decision-makers and other actors to implement consistent policies on awareness raising, prevention and appropriate punitive measures for combating everyday violence. These policies will be formulated and applied in a manner which respects human rights and the rule of law. Only then can the conditions and feelings about security in Europe be improved on a permanent basis.

*The prevention of violence in sport* is the first of a series of publications designed to acquaint the reader with recommendations or instruments used to launch Council of Europe activities and projects on violence prevention. The series also includes analytical and summary documents on the different themes covered by this integrated project.

# CONTENTS

*Page*

**Foreword**
*Walter Schwimmer, Secretary General of the Council of Europe* ........... 7

**Introduction** ................................................................. 9

**I. General principles behind a prevention policy** .................... 11
*The current situation as regards hooliganism* .............................. 11
Football clubs and leagues ..................................................... 11
International tournaments involving national teams ...................... 12

*Need for preventive measures to combat violence in sport* ............. 13
Utility of social and educational coaching of fans ......................... 14
Importance of good hospitality and escorting of spectators at
sports events ...................................................................... 15
Need for improved club-supporter relations and for strengthening
of clubs' social role ............................................................. 17
Need for local authority involvement ........................................ 18

**II. Initiatives and preventive measures** ............................... 19
*Fan coaching* ..................................................................... 19
The method ........................................................................ 19
The targets ........................................................................ 23
The staff involved ............................................................... 23
Relations between fan coaching schemes and the police ................ 24
International co-operation in the field of fan coaching ................... 25

*Fan embassies* ................................................................... 27
Concept and background ....................................................... 27
Goals ................................................................................ 27
Functioning ........................................................................ 28
Finance ............................................................................. 37

*Accompanying persons* ........................................................ 38
Role and tasks .................................................................... 38
Structure ........................................................................... 39
Recruitment, selection and training .......................................... 39
National and international co-ordination .................................... 40

*Relations between clubs and supporters* .................................................. 41
Supporters' charter .................................................................................. 41
Club officials responsible for supporter relations and associations
of fans ...................................................................................................... 41
Supporters' departments ......................................................................... 42
*The club's role in its social environment* ............................................... 42
Working with the community ................................................................. 42
The city at the stadium and the stadium in the city ................................ 44
*The role of local authorities* .................................................................. 44
Educational activities .............................................................................. 44
The need for a "contractual commitment": the role of advisory
committees for the prevention of violence in sport ................................ 45
Activities for local people during international tournaments ................. 46

**Conclusion** ........................................................................................... 49

**Bibliography** ....................................................................................... 51

## Foreword

Preventing and combating everyday violence is today, in all our member states, a key political concern. In a democratic society any policy in this sphere, in whatever field, hinges first and foremost on collective awareness of the causes of violence and the dangers it presents to fundamental values and social cohesion.

It is only through concerted and coherent action that we can take up the challenge. Partnership between all those concerned (political and administrative authorities, civil society, education, police, judges, social services, etc.) has to be, in my eyes, one of the central principles of any policy pursued.

In addition to reiterating these general fundamental principles, I think it essential that the Council of Europe assists member states in implementing more specific initiatives in certain places or particularly sensitive areas.

Sport is a means of bringing people and social groups together, particularly as it uses rules and traditions to channel aggression, focusing it on the goal to be achieved and on healthy emulation and competition rather than violent conflict.

Even so, some terribly tragic events have deeply marked Europe's collective consciousness in recent times. We all remember the Heysel stadium tragedy and other serious incidents that took place at European or world sporting events. Sadly, these very spectacular calamities are only one aspect of a far deeper phenomenon seen in various sports and at all levels, be it professional or amateur, international, national or local.

This publication is a remarkable analytical summary of the problems and causes and also of proposals for activities and initiatives to be implemented at local level. I hope that it will be welcomed by all its intended readers as a basis for discussion and action for the future.

*Walter Schwimmer*
*Secretary General of the Council of Europe*

## Introduction

The prevention of violence is a concept that has become inextricably linked with sports events in every country of Europe. The concept nevertheless takes many forms and corresponds to widely differing realities in practice.

Preventive activities vary widely, ranging from evening remedial lessons for child supporters run by football clubs to adventure sport activities organised for hooligans at weekends and to the well-publicised fan embassies at major tournaments and fair-play campaigns. Some activities are also organised by associations on private initiative, and still more are run under government programmes carried out by official public institutions.

These schemes as a whole prove highly useful and are definitely effective, although the philosophies behind them and the political lines which they follow vary. This is a good thing, for humankind derives much of its interest from people's differences, and social progress stems from diversity. It is nevertheless necessary to ensure that prevention policy is consistent and that activities on the ground are placed on a sound basis. The policy adopted to prevent violence at sports events therefore necessitates a consistent structure and a harmonious framework at international level.

The experience acquired could be turned to greater advantage, and a consistent approach maintained to the prevention of spectator violence, if a reference document was made available in the form of a prevention study, covering the ways of putting projects such as "fan embassies" into practice, the basic methods to be used to ensure that a common approach is taken to fan coaching, and ideas for action with a view to a joined-up prevention policy within a club or a local authority.

These are the initial – liberal and ambitious – thoughts underlying this study on the prevention of violence at sports events, the more realistic aim of which is, nevertheless, to make a modest contribution to the management of spectator violence at European football grounds by attempting to add one more brick to the complex building – still under construction – of tolerance in sport, both amateur and professional.

## I. GENERAL PRINCIPLES BEHIND A PREVENTION POLICY

**The current situation as regards hooliganism**

In this early part of the 21st century, violence at football grounds remains a disturbing problem, one which is still extremely topical, in spite of all the efforts made and resources invested over the past twenty years or so. Every country in Europe is affected. While the problem takes different forms, it is equally acute everywhere.

The general situation has been stabilising, while violence has been shifting from inside football grounds to outside, including urban areas and city centres, and those involved in such violence have also changed, with the role of football fans tending to be played now by young people from difficult neighbourhoods, and with hooliganism becoming linked to urban violence.

*Football clubs and leagues*

*Spontaneous one-off instances of violence*

Violence has occurred at football grounds ever since football became a spectator sport, namely since the end of the 19th century in England and the early years of the 20th on the mainland. This violence is of a spontaneous nature involving the whole body of supporters. The potential is there for the majority of spectators to be dragged into this kind of violence, depending on the circumstances and on the interplay between a combination of risk factors and emotional reactions. This spontaneous violence is not confined to professional football, but occurs widely in the amateur game both among spectators and among players.

*Organised permanent violence*

The contemporary football world faces permanent violence of a "premeditated" kind. This is group violence, in the form of physical aggression or vandalism, engaged in by hard-core groups of supporters, commonly regarded as hooligans, in the context of a sort of "competition" running in parallel with the rivalry between their football teams. These hard-core groups follow a particular club and systematically seek confrontation with their counterparts from each rival club. They regard themselves as elite supporters and their membership of a group of hooligans as a "way of life" which helps to add value to their social identity.

This violence may take a relatively organised form, in that the hooligans do have a certain level of structuring. It is premeditated in the sense that it is pre-planned, and usually expected on a given day. This is why numerous incidents occur prior to matches. It also has to be said that the hard-core groups make use of new communications technologies (GSM, the Internet, and so on) when planning and carrying out their acts of violence.

*Football disasters*

The earliest date at which the first major football disaster can be considered to have occurred was 1902 (when twenty-five spectators died in Glasgow, where a stand collapsed), and disasters have continued to mark the history of the sport, with certain names becoming sadly famous, European examples being Bolton, Sheffield, Bradford and Bastia, not forgetting, of course, the Heysel stadium disaster. More recent disasters in South Africa and Ghana now have to be added to the list.

As detailed studies have shown, most such disasters stem from problems of defective infrastructure, inadequate organisation (sale of too many tickets, and spectator areas with insufficient capacity) or poor organisation, or even contributory action, of the security staff. It is now possible to take the view that, if national legislation and security regulations are complied with, and if the recommendations made in the European Convention on Spectator Violence and Misbehaviour at Sports Events and in Particular at Football Matches (ETS No. 120) are strictly applied, this kind of disaster can now be avoided (although an area of doubt remains as regards ticket management, especially where international tournaments are concerned, because a black market exists).

*International tournaments involving national teams*

International tournaments are one-off large-scale events where considerable spectator movements and a significant crowd have to be managed over a fairly lengthy period of time.

Empirical analysis and various field studies at this level have revealed the profile of national teams' supporters to differ from that of club fans. The average age of the spectators tends to be higher, crowd behaviour is more disci-

*General principles behind a prevention policy*

plined, and the spectators tend to be better off, so better-dressed and behaved. It has also been noted that a far greater proportion of women attend such matches, a phenomenon which started in the Scandinavian countries and has spread, especially in France, where the "World Cup effect" played an important role.

However, there are two noteworthy exceptions: England and Germany. While the majority of their supporters are convivial and believe in fair play, hooligans also travel in large numbers on the European territory and are repeatedly responsible for serious incidents. As a result, exceptional security, crowd control and policing measures have to be taken. It should also be noted that virtually no incidents occur inside football grounds during such tournaments, most incidents happening in city centres, sometimes even in the intervals between matches.

**Need for preventive measures to combat violence in sport**

A huge amount of work has been done since the Heysel tragedy, both within states and through international co-operation, relating to police activity, infrastructure, spectator control and video monitoring, organisation (ticketing) and legislation. In contrast, while many initiatives have been launched at local level to prevent violence and to take educational or social action, much remains to be done at international level, especially at European level.

In order to supplement conventional security measures and to ensure that they are balanced, the overall international policy on hooligan management must place a greater emphasis on prevention and step up its efforts in this field.

As events give rise to distinct situations and the supporters present different profiles, there needs to be a specifically different approach to preventive activity for league and club matches, on the one hand, and international tournaments involving national teams, on the other, implying different kinds of responses and appropriate structures for action.

Where long-term league championships are concerned, preventive activity in Europe must involve detailed work over the medium and longer term, through the stimulation, development and, where they already exist, strengthening of educational and social activities aimed at supporters, so that the problem can be overcome and violence can gradually be brought to an end. On the occasion of the actual matches, there is also a need for support to be given to security efforts and event management through shorter-term action making use of preventive skills based on mediation and communication methods. Prevention must be targeted at supporters, but must also take into account clubs' environment and must involve local authorities in the process.

When international football tournaments are held, security management needs to be supplemented by appropriate preventive action based on the use of "accompanying persons" who travel with supporters and on a hospitality policy backed by specialised facilities to help visiting supporters.

At national level, overall consistency must be achieved in prevention policy, and support must be given to local initiatives, by bringing together the institutions concerned and the parties involved in management of the problem in a permanent structure. Spain and Portugal have followed the English example by setting up a national council against violence in sport, while France has its joint national committee on stadium security at football league level, and Germany has a national committee on sport and security, in which its Association of Towns and Cities, the German Sports Federation, the Youth and Sport Ministry, the Fan Project Co-ordination Office and the National Football Federation participate, among others.

*Utility of social and educational coaching of fans*

When it was realised that hooligans were constantly changing strategy, getting involved in increasingly sophisticated action, and that incidents were shifting outside football grounds, thought began to be given in several countries to the need to take drastic educational action over the longer term.

It also became apparent that hooligans were proving their symbolic worth through their acts of violence and their involvement in a hard core under the media spotlight. Rather than anonymity or a lack of identity, hooligans prefer the negative identity derived from their membership of a violent group involved in incidents that receive large amounts of media attention.

It became clear that it was necessary to ask social workers to carry out educational activities targeted specifically at supporters, and several countries took steps towards this end. Supplementing both passive security measures connected with infrastructure or supervision and police action to manage events, fan coaching is part of an operational prevention policy extending over the medium and long term, based on fundamental ongoing work with supporters.

The institutions which support a fan coaching policy require a full dose of political courage, for the work is difficult and very much centred on quality, so it is not a very high profile task, and the results only emerge over the longer term.

*Importance of good hospitality and escorting of spectators at sports events*

The fundamental idea underlying organisation of a sports event must be the priority given to spectator and public safety: security should prevail over financial interests. Thus the major challenge during sports events is that of striking a balance between the strict requirements of security in the light of actual risk factors and the need to maintain the festive and convivial nature of the event.

The event must remain a welcoming and festive one, with local and foreign fans being treated correctly and with respect. As far as hospitality during matches is concerned, there is a need for a consistent approach to fan coaching, to the reception facilities organised for them and to the transport and accommodation policy adopted.

Experience has shown that an integrated view of security policies enables possible spectator excesses to be kept to a minimum, while allowing the event to continue to offer a festival of football. And a multidisciplinary approach is vital, both to the planning and preparation of the event and to its practical organisation and arrangements. There is no miracle solution, nor is there a single way. A number of converging measures are needed, encompassing the various repressive, structuring and preventive dimensions, through ongoing consultations between all who are concerned, particularly between police and prevention services. This partnership requires a consensus among all concerned and their involvement from the planning stage and during the event.

An integrated prevention policy for international tournaments needs to be placed in an international framework, with constant interaction between the different levels of responsibility and sectors of action. Prevention must aim first and foremost to offer the best possible arrangements for receiving all foreign supporters. The concept of hospitality is the main, unavoidable, thread which must be followed by both police action and prevention arrangements.

It is important to note that the work done before matches take place, in the hours and even days preceding games, is vital. Events preceding matches invariably have an effect on supporter behaviour and on the atmosphere in the ground.

Complementing this work, the efforts made must be focused not only on supporters, but also on preparing the local population. Local people not only help to welcome visiting supporters and to create a convivial atmosphere, lending the tournament its "magic", making it unique and incomparable with other kinds of major event, but also play an important role in the success of the tournament, and they have a vital part to play both at the ground and in the city.

At the same time, the tournament must not generate a feeling of exclusion, especially in what are described as disadvantaged neighbourhoods or among "problem" young people. Specific activities need to be organised, especially in conjunction with the associations already working in these urban areas and experienced in dealing with the members of the public concerned. The World Cup in France and Euro 2000 showed that connections are being established between urban violence and the world of football. Young people from neighbourhoods described as difficult found a role in these events by attacking foreign supporters, especially English fans, and created additional difficulties for the management of the tournament outside the context of the matches.

It should be noted that the hard core of local hooligans definitely presents a risk factor. The event may place them in potential conflict situations that they can exploit, as well as with media coverage enabling them to increase their profile and reputation in the context of an event that is taking place on "their" territory. Appropriate preventive action closely focused on these members of the hard core in specific geographical areas, of the kind organised in Liège during Euro 2000, enables the activities of this kind of group to be channelled and the risks to be very much reduced.

A fundamental aim of the prevention arrangements is to complement the work done by the police, *inter alia,* by relieving the police of some of their overload of work in respect of the secondary task of providing public information, thus enabling them to concentrate on their priority tasks of maintaining order. The prevention programme also plays a significant role in creating a calm atmosphere and hence limiting the number of situations that might potentially require police action.

Management of an international sporting competition requires preventive arrangements encompassing all supporters, but also, and in particular, extending to city centres. The approach has changed considerably, with numerous experiments being carried out along the way. Each country has made its contribution to the new concept that has been born, hospitality and "accompanying persons" who escort fans, something that is now always arranged by the organisers, and ensures the success of any tournament. The schemes run by associations, and even by ordinary people, such as the Football Supporters' Association's (FSA) successful project during Euro 96, and the convivial philosophy created by the French government for the 1998 World Cup led the way towards the implementation during Euro 2000, for the first time by public authorities, of a prevention programme aimed directly at supporters, involving permanent stationary facilities, such as the "fan embassies", and mobile partners such as the "accompanying persons", while, at the same time due account was taken of the need to provide activities for the local population.

It has proven useful to give a free hand to the local tier, and particularly to city authorities, for the implementation of proximity arrangements, and to make the national tier responsible for general co-ordination, management of the programme and logistical support.

*Need for improved club-supporter relations and for strengthening of clubs' social role*

Football plays an integral part in society and cannot survive detached from the world around it. It is vital that existing relationships should be strengthened and new ones be created or recreated between the world of sport, including football, and the general environment, reaching both supporters and associations or local authorities. There is a dimension common to the world of football and the world in the sense of our planet, and this must remain.

The impact of the environment can play a significant role. Supporters' culture provides them with a reference framework directly influencing their behaviour. We note that certain countries, such as Scotland and the Scandinavian countries, have developed a "positive culture" for their national supporters, turning them into veritable ambassadors of tolerance and fair play. This is sometimes done in a structured way, as in Denmark, where the "Fair Fans" programme is intended to promote dialogue between supporters and to sustain positive relations between the supporters of rival clubs. In Germany some very emblematic figures (extremely popular, top-level sportsmen and -women) assume the role of "national sports ambassadors" for tolerance and fair play.

The crowd is an integral part of the spectacle that sport provides, and spectators make a contribution to the way in which sport operates and continues to develop.

Sport is changing, football in particular, in a way that is placing an ever greater distance between the clubs and their audience. The usual view taken of the spectator is a commercial one, for spectators are consumer items, or rather passive consumers of an item (the spectator sport) and of all that is associated with it, whereas, paradoxically, fan culture is active, involving the individual and being highly emotionally charged. The result is a decreasing sense of responsibility among spectators *vis-à-vis* the sporting institution, which is perceived as an abstract entity.

A recent phenomenon in every corner of Europe, from Marseilles to Istanbul, via Liège, Florence and Rotterdam, has been large-scale movements challenging developments, coupled with violent demands, leading to attacks by supporters on club management or players.

Some supporters or clubs have been taking action to increase the sense of responsibility, as has been the case in Azerbaijan, where a union of Neftchi fans, based in Baku, has been set up in the form of an association and organises travel for fans, also offering support to both clubs and the police in match management and ground security.

There seems to be a vital need for sports clubs and organisations to adopt a stronger fan support policy, thus starting a process by which they draw closer to their fans, forging a new social link.

*Need for local authority involvement*

By their very nature, local authorities have a major role to play in policy for preventing violence in sport. The lowest tier of public institutions, particularly city councils, need to be catalysts in prevention policies and to give impetus to activities involving sports organisations or associations. The local tier is the ideal level for developing consultations between partners on the ground, but also for running activities linked to concrete problems. To ensure effective co-operation, geared to meeting tangible needs, local authority involvement must result in contractual commitments regarding prevention policies.

## II. INITIATIVES AND PREVENTIVE MEASURES

**Fan coaching**

Fan coaching is part of an effort described as one of "offensive socio-prevention", for it is carried out wherever the target audience is and requires a proactive approach. Fan coaching involves a mobile effort, both home and away, also encompassing ongoing educational and social work during the periods of supporters' lives when they are not involved in football, thanks to the organisation of structured educational activities. The most structured and institutionalised efforts in terms of fan coaching have mainly been made in Germany, the Netherlands and Belgium.

The Standing Committee of the European Convention on Spectator Violence closely examined the question of educational and social work among young supporters as long ago as 1992, with a study of the fan coaching method. In practice fan coaching is conducted according to different philosophies, mainly because supporters have different profiles, but also because hooliganism itself differs as well, leading to the adoption in each country of different methods of action. This means of action accordingly offers a range of practical approaches. Fan coaching must be a flexible concept, so as to be adaptable to each situation on the ground, according to local needs and specific national cultures.

As regards responsibilities and funding, governments have a role to play, with direct support from clubs and local authorities concerning the organisational aspects and implementation.

*The method*

Fan coaching takes place on match days, using a situation-based approach, but also, and above all, during the rest of the week, through educational and social activity which is ongoing.

*Match days*

When fan-coaching services are provided by staff recognised by the institutions and accepted by the fans, the centre ground can be occupied, and preventive action can be taken on the spot when potentially dangerous situations arise.

The staff mediates between fans and police, and between fans and club stewards or security staff. Thanks both to their special position at the heart of events and to constant dialogue, they are able to defuse some conflicts and thereby help to avoid certain incidents.

The main aim is to ensure that a channel of communication is open between supporters and organisers.

*Educational activities*

The educational activities take place during the week and provide an opportunity to carry out specifically targeted educational work with supporters outside the particular context of matches and the excitement associated with them.

The organisation of classic sporting activities (such as football on a full-sized or smaller pitch) as part of an educational project to involve young people and make them more responsible is also intended to prevent young supporters from finding themselves at a loose end in their cities, while at the same time enabling them to meet their need to be active. Some structure is offered through participation in amateur championships.

Adventure sports, such as rafting, canyoning, climbing, and so on, prove very appropriate, enabling young supporters to prove their worth in a positive field, by meeting open-air sporting challenges, rather than through resorting to violence. They also enable young people to expend their pent-up energy, while providing them with the excitement they need. Significantly, they learn proper standards by participating in this kind of activities.

As the key to these efforts is the inculcation of responsibility and the achievement of involvement, offering supporters consumer activities merely to keep them occupied is to be avoided, for the essential aim is to enable young supporters' positive resources and potential to be brought into play and to express themselves through action.

*Social support*

When a relay function is fulfilled and individual attention given, individuals with social difficulties who are not helped by conventional institutions can be given assistance. When fans' social situations are improved, one step is

*Initiatives and preventive measures*

High mountain climbing with fixed supports (via ferrata) with young fans from violent groups (Massif des Ecrins, France). Courtesy of the Fan Coaching Association, Liège (Belgium).

Canyoning in Haut Allier (France) with young fans from violent groups. Courtesy of the Fan Coaching Association, Liège (Belgium).

thereby taken towards making them more individually independent. The link with football means that there is an opportunity here to carry out social work targeted at certain disadvantaged groups.

*Street work or educational infrastructure (Fan home)*

Permanent contact with fans is important, providing the cement which binds the educational work which needs to be done. Such contact may be maintained through street work carried out in residential neighbourhoods or on premises frequented by fans, such as bars, keeping in contact with them between matches and activities, and enabling a relationship of trust to develop. Or it may take the form of a fan centre, an educational infrastructure open during the week and offering games and educational material, providing a place where fans can meet each other freely in an educational context. This kind of infrastructure provides a permanent interface between fan coaching and fans.

*The targets*

The initial aim of fan coaching is to target supporters described as being "risks", especially the young fringe of potential offenders. Certain projects target category C supporters (permanent, hard-core hooliganism), while others target category B (traditional supporters, presenting an occasional risk of violence). The selected targets are very much determined by the local situation and by the nature of the hard core groups. It is very difficult to target category C at certain clubs, as they are ultra-specialised in violence.

*The staff involved*

It is vital for such activities to be carried out by teams of professionals specialising in social or educational work, steeped in the supporters' culture and working among the fans. The skills used and the professional way in which the task is carried out are vital, because of the sensitive area in which the activities are conducted and the complexity of the psycho-social problems involved. "Fan coaches" must work under an employment contract, and their intervention in the specific area of football must be part of a broader prevention or urban security programme implemented at municipal level.

*Relations between fan coaching schemes and the police*

Fan coaching taking place in a context of integrated prevention is of proven effectiveness. A partitioned approach might give rise to effects that are the opposite of these expected. Positive co-operation between the police and "fan coaches" is vital to a long-term structured prevention policy. While the methods differ, the objectives are identical: to reduce violence in sport.

If a project is to be successful, it is vital that both partners should be kept fully informed in advance about the methodology, objectives and nature of the activities. Everyone's role must be well defined. It is also important for information on fan coaching to be provided to those members of the police force who are on duty during matches. The time and energy spent on this preliminary phase represent an investment which will immediately pay dividends, thanks to the effectiveness of the action taken on the spot, for which good co-operation between fan coaches and the police is absolutely essential.

Official consultation structures are needed, where exchanges and dialogue can take place about respective practice, and these should be co-ordinated by the local authority. Experience has shown that, as well as facilitating co-operation in the field, such consultation is mutually beneficial to both partners. An exchange to which different viewpoints are contributed improves the potential and the professional practice of each party.

Fan coaches must accept that police work is useful to society and take the view that spectator safety is a priority, which can be successfully guaranteed only if the police keep order. In this context it is important for "fan coaches" not to align themselves against institutions and not to fall into the role of the supporters' "trade union", something which would create great confusion.

It is vital for members of the police force to acknowledge the significant contribution to keeping quiet those spectators who pose a risk that is made by the educational work done by fan coaches, whom they must recognise as full partners. One important thing in this context is for the usefulness in relation to individual and group behaviour of the educational work carried out over the longer term to be recognised, and another is for the effectiveness of social work in achieving a positive solution to problem situations to be appreciated by the police.

In practical terms, it is useful for a police representative to be involved, in an advisory capacity, in the work of the fan coaching management committee. At the same time, we note that some experiments in which fan coaching was integrated into policing structures have produced negative results. Fan coaching must not be placed under police supervision.

A sensitive area is that of information. Fan coaches, thanks to their special position on the streets and among supporters during matches, are able to cast useful light on the context of a match, a stadium or the atmosphere within a group of supporters, and can provide general information needed to improve security management. However, such information must never be of an individual nature, and fan coaches must never work as informers or do the same work as police "spotters".

*International co-operation in the field of fan coaching*

With both football and hooliganism now having an international dimension, the fan coaching approach should be extended to other European countries, according to local needs.

It is vital that a fan coaching working method should be developed in Europe which has at least some common features and is relatively standardised, so that international socio-prevention policy can be made consistent, but also, and particularly, so as to make sure that operational co-operation in the field is effective, especially when cup matches between European clubs take place.

It is essential for there to be a common general framework for the various fan coaching schemes in Europe, as well as a number of common features among the principles for action in the field. Nevertheless, as each country, region and city has its own peculiarities, activities must be tailored to these specific local features, in particular as regards the level of institutionalisation and dialogue between fan coaches and the police.

The basic principle is one of aggressive social and educational action in the field by skilled professionals who work in a targeted manner, focusing on groups of young football fans. It is essential to develop projects continually, ensuring that new staff are constantly brought in and provided with in-service training, so that activities do not become bogged down in tradition. The supporters' world is changing, so, by definition, fan-coaching projects must also develop in practice.

Fan coaching schemes are qualitative background activities that take on their full scope when they are part of the local environment, and they must largely be run within a club or a city.

International relations between fan coaching schemes should focus more on exchanges of specific experience, so as to reinforce and enrich each country's practice.

There is a need for local fan coaching activities to be interlinked via a national platform, which itself should have a link with an international co-ordination body which ensures that information circulates and that the necessary consultations take place. Thus each country should appoint a national fan-coaching correspondent to centralise information and disseminate it both locally and internationally.

The effort to introduce international fan coaching activities should therefore move towards an "international fan coaching platform", in the form of a forum for exchange, consultations and communication between national projects, also intended to guarantee that a common framework for action exists. This would offer an opportunity for empirical analyses of the problems associated with fan philosophy in the various countries and could also facilitate information exchange when European inter-club matches are to be held for which fan-coaching schemes are to take their traditional preventive action.

At the same time, the participation of fan coaching projects in a broader international exchange programme designed to prevent hooliganism, extended to other types of prevention, is a positive element in the strengthening of European prevention policy. When fan coaching schemes are set up in new countries, they should draw on the experience already gained by the first countries to adopt such schemes.

Fan coaching is a concept that is primarily aimed at club supporters. The significant difference between the context of inter-club fixtures and matches between national teams, as well as the different profiles of national team and club fans, prompt us to avoid mingling the two approaches, which correspond to distinct professional tasks. An international fan coaching structure for fans of national teams should focus more on the concept of the use of "accompanying persons" (see "accompanying persons" p. xxx), a concept that is more flexible and enables the work done to extend to all supporters. While the "accompanying persons" may include some workers from the fan coaching schemes, not all should come from that source.

## Fan embassies

*Concept and background*

The concept of fan embassies dates back to the initiatives taken by the Football Supporters Association (FSA) at various tournaments abroad, and subsequently by the KOS (German co-ordination of fan projects), in the form of mobile embassies specifically targeted at their national supporters. The system that operated best and was most successful was used during the 1998 World Cup in France, involving mobile English and German fan embassies (in the form of mini-buses), vehicles that accompanied their supporters to the various host cities. It should be noted that the Netherlands and Belgium sent accompanying persons to Euro 92 in Sweden and to the 1990 World Cup in Italy respectively. When Euro 96 took place, the FSA took the initiative of setting up fan embassies in some of the host cities, and fan consulates near to certain grounds.

These practical experiments were positively evaluated in a scientific study carried out prior to Euro 2000 by the University of Liège, which did its research between 1997 and 2000. Research workers recommended that the authorities of both host countries adopt the scheme. These specific and innovative preventive practices were identified as being positive, adaptable and transposable at international seminars held to look at security at international tournaments. These were attended by parties with a prevention role and organised by the European Forum for Urban Security in Liège in 1998 and in St Denis in 1999, by the Belgian Secretariat for Prevention Policy and the Franco-German youth office in Brussels in 1999, by the Ministry for Health, Welfare and Sport in Eindhoven and Rotterdam (Netherlands) in 1999, and by the British Council and the Council of Europe in Strasbourg in 1999.

The upshot of all these efforts was the definition by the Dutch and Belgian governments of a joint prevention programme, as well as the taking of an official policy decision on the carrying out of a large-scale preventive campaign for Euro 2000, with appropriate funding. Fan embassies were set up in each host city, with the help of skilled staff from various sectors.

*Goals*

Fan embassies in principle are intended to offer a fixed point to which foreign supporters can go, and they focus on fan culture and on supporters' specific needs during the tournament. They provide supporters with an opportunity to talk in their own language to officials familiar with the supporters' specific environment, and who have the necessary skills to solve their individual difficulties. Fans can also obtain information and assistance relating to matches, to ticket sales, to accommodation, to travel, to leisure activities, to any planned screenings of matches, to the theft or loss of documents and to health care, and a wide variety of information about such matters as currency exchange or alternative activities.

The aim is thus to provide a conduit, or a permanent channel of communication, between supporters and the local and national authorities, particularly so that up-to-date information can be rapidly and efficiently disseminated, for a tournament, by definition, has a life of its own and can undergo constant change, with situations altering considerably and speedily. As the tournament itself is not fixed and immoveable, it is essential to have a facility directly linked to the situation in the field, and able to adapt to changing situations.

Fan embassies provide an official and efficient link between national authorities, the authorities of host cities, the tournament organiser and the whole body of supporters.

*Functioning*

The key requirement is that the structure should be capable of dealing with supporters in an appropriate manner, in particular fans of visiting teams. The degree of professionalism and the structure's autonomy differ according to national cultural tendencies. Fan embassies are sometimes set up by the organising public authorities or alternatively by the supporters themselves.

*Structure*

During any international tournament, each host city should have its own fan embassy scheme. Various formats are possible: a single embassy, or two embassies – one for each of the countries concerned – possibly even with a third information centre for other foreign fans in transit.

Each model has its own advantages and drawbacks. A decision therefore needs to be taken in the light of situations and specific local features as to whether each city should have one or two fan embassies. The main thing is for the idea of setting up such a facility to be put into practice in accordance with high quality standards.

*Staffing and human resources*

It is preferable for the staff taken on for the duration of the event to be both paid and skilled and to have a contract with an institutional authority or an officially appointed association, enabling the arrangements to operate in a professional manner, ensuring that the nature of the tasks carried out is monitored and providing a guarantee that everything is on an official basis.

By way of example, a fan embassy may include the following members of staff:

- one general co-ordinator with a local prevention role, who has an overview of all the facilities set up and is in direct and permanent contact with the local authorities and the national support unit;
- one fan embassy co-ordinator from the fan project, where such a project exists, or from a supporters' association. This person needs to have a link with fan culture or with sporting or youth culture;
- one staff member from the city's prevention department, if such a department exists, or from the sport/youth department, or at least from a local official public service;
- a permanent staff member recruited specifically for the duration of the tournament (selected as having organisational and management ability and for a knowledge of the most widely-spoken foreign languages, such as English, French, and so forth);
- one bilingual translator per visiting country (languages of the host and the visiting countries), taken on specifically for the days preceding and following the matches of the country concerned;
- one diplomat representing the official embassy of the visiting country;
- one official delegate of the private organiser or the sports federation concerned;
- two "accompanying persons" from the visiting country.

It is also possible for the team to include a police officer from the prevention department (acting as a relay and as a provider of information), a representative of the tourist office and a member of the Red Cross.

When these staff are available, joint teams can be set up covering different skills and specialisations, and of different national and linguistic origins. It is vital for the staff from the host country to work hand in hand with those from the visiting country.

*Opening hours*

Fan embassies must of course be physically accessible, and it must be possible to contact them by telephone during a maximum number of hours. Experience has shown that permanent opening throughout the tournament is necessary, with minimum staffing during the slack periods. On the other hand, the embassies must be open for as long as possible (9 a.m. to midnight) on the day before, the day of and the day after each match. One of the advantages of fan embassies is their accessibility, and another is their flexibility, enabling them to adapt to the situations that arise and also to tailor their activities to the lifestyles of visiting supporters.

*Location and access*

Choosing a location is a sensitive part of the preparations, as fan embassies must, in practice, be accessible, visible and in a place that is easy to get to, but must not overcrowd areas where there would already be huge numbers of people, cause congestion which would be difficult to manage or interfere with the flow of traffic. An effort also needs to be made to avoid proximity with what are described as risk areas or areas frequented by groups with criminal tendencies.

This question of location, more than any other, needs to be the subject of close consultation between prevention services, supporters' associations, police and local authority, in the light of specific local characteristics, so that a consensus is reached which takes account of all the parameters. Ideally, it is useful for fan embassies to be located in city centres, enabling a considerable amount of work to be done in advance of the match and making the embassies accessible to the greatest possible numbers, for supporters as a whole traditionally go to the ground only an hour or two before kick-off.

In addition, the quality of the fan reception infrastructure and the surrounding environment symbolise the level of the host city's commitment to welcoming fans and offering them hospitality. It is useful, as was done at Euro 96, to set up a fan consulate near the ground, so that supporters have an alternative point of reference during the periods immediately before and after each match.

The way to fan embassies must be indicated by means of effective and visible signs, making it easy for supporters to find them and making them accessible at any time. The signs must contain a logo which is common to all the host cities, making identification easier. The literature distributed to supporters in their own countries before the tournament must give the addresses and other details of the fan embassies. An interesting idea is to print special posters with huge city maps showing the location of fan embassies (and other useful information such as where to find bus stops, cash dispensers, etc.) for display in the windows of shops and cafes, enabling supporters anywhere and at any time to establish their own location or to find out where their fan embassies are.

*Reception facilities, services and information*

All supporters need to be able to obtain assistance or full, appropriate and up-to-date information about matches and the tournament, ticketing, accommodation, travel, loss of documents, health care, cultural or alternative activities, and so on. Efficient dissemination of information is a major contributor to preventive action in the management of international tournaments.

As fan embassy staff are in constant touch with the organiser, local and national authorities, the police and the security services, they are able to provide supporters with up-to-date and accurate information. They must make sure that this information is definite and reliable, and constantly check its accuracy, so that no misleading information is provided to supporters.

An associated aim is to nip rumours in the bud. The widest variety of quite fantastic rumours circulate among supporters during tournaments, and these may create difficulties that are not easy to deal with. As fan embassies combine an official position at the heart of the network of organising bodies with special and immediate relationships with supporters on the spot, they are able rapidly and definitively to put a stop to this kind of rumour.

It is vital for each fan embassy to have available information, maps and leaflets relating to the other host cities, so that these can be distributed to supporters in advance.

*Matches and arrangements for the tournament*

Fan embassies distribute brochures containing information about football grounds, their location, access to them, local public transport and the kick-off times of matches. This information must include legislation as it relates to the tournament or to crowd management and the rules applied within each ground, including any items that are prohibited. While it is obvious that a number of portable items are banned (such as weapons or blunt instruments), it is less obvious whether others are prohibited, as regulations vary from country to country and even from match to match, where items such as cameras, mobile telephones, video cameras and umbrellas are concerned. Fans may also be uncertain about some items used as part of their national fan culture, such as fireworks. It is vital that fans should be informed at an early enough stage of these provisions, so that frustration and tension are avoided at the ground.

Information must also be provided about the legislation governing the black market.

*Tickets and their distribution*

Ticket sales are a matter for the organisers and are managed at that level.

Information must be made available about pricing, sales outlets, the numbers of tickets remaining and the time limits and conditions applying to sales. It is important for fans to be told at a sufficiently early stage – and to know that this information is reliable – when a match has been sold out, how many tickets are still available and at what prices, or when ticket sales have finished, and so on.

The presence of an official delegate from the organisers is necessary, as is permanent telephone and electronic contact with the organiser's office.

The black market in tickets is a recurrent problem. The black market is part of the fan culture during international tournaments, short-circuiting all the measures taken to keep supporters apart inside and around the grounds. Experience has shown that, in view of the nature and profile of national teams' followers, the resultant mingling has not caused problems or given rise to major incidents during tournaments, but the separation of people regarded as rival fans underlies the security arrangements and is a statutory obligation. If there is specific legislation outlawing the black market for a tournament, it is vital that fan embassies should refrain from participating in any distribution of tickets via the black market and from transmitting information about parallel sales circuits. This is important, for the privileged position and central role of fan embassies make them favoured targets for black market ticket sellers, who regard them as easy and efficient sales channels.

*Initiatives and preventive measures*

Danish fans celebrating at the Fan Embassy at Liège during Euro 2000. Courtesy of the Fan Coaching Association, Liège (Belgium).

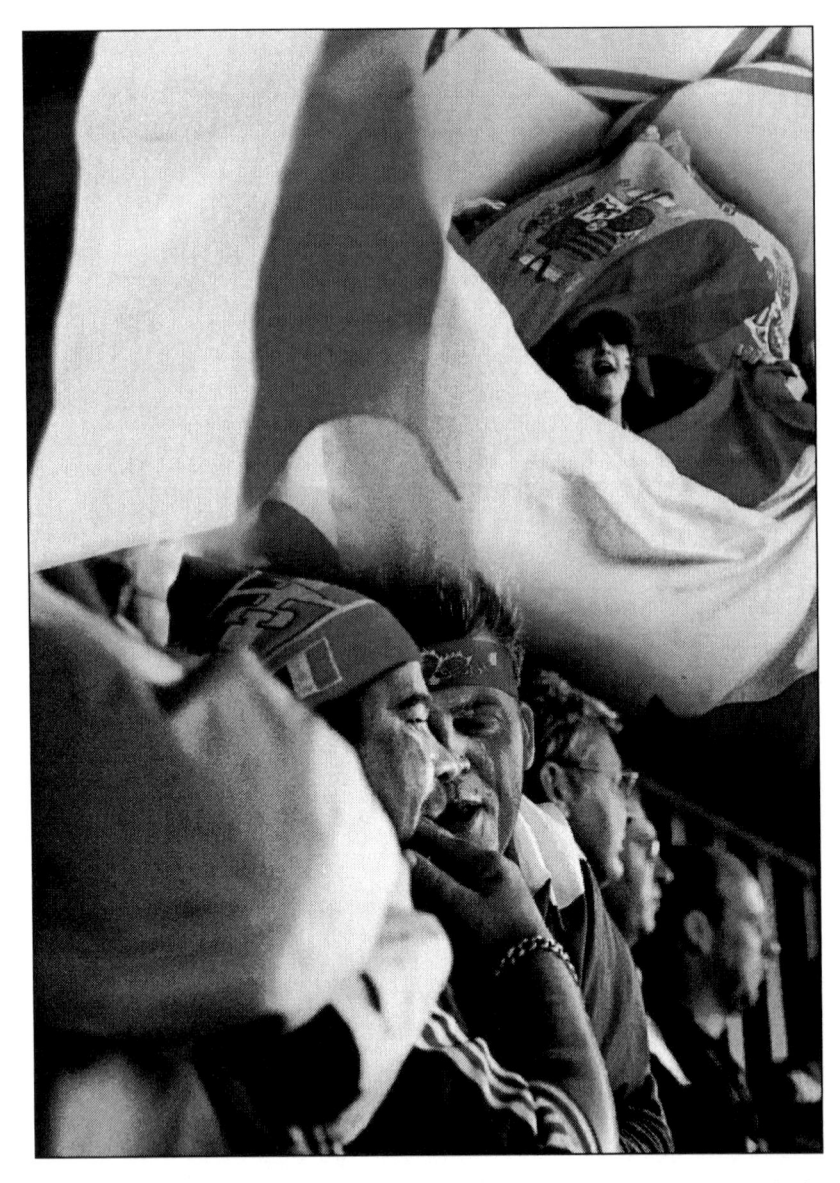

Multicultural photo montage of fans from different countries during Euro 2000, Netherlands-Belgium. Courtesy of the Secrétariat permanent à la politique de prévention, ministère de l'Intérieur, Brussels (Belgium).

*Accommodation*

Generally speaking, fan embassies complement or back up conventional tourist offices, which provide information about ordinary accommodation and services. It is important that information should be provided not only about ordinary hotels, but also about more economical accommodation, such as campsites or bed and breakfast establishments, and accurate information should also be supplied about public transport services to these places (location, cost and timetable).

The accommodation problem is often very acute in some cities, where critical situations may lead to tension or disorder. Either the number of places available is too low, or thousands of supporters arrive unexpectedly at a place that is off the beaten tourist track. Fan embassies deal with this kind of problem, in conjunction with the local authority. Similarly, when all accommodation is taken, supporters must be able to be pointed towards more distant accommodation and told about the means of transport they can use to get there. When more critical cases arise, fan embassies may, in consultation with the security services, organise and orchestrate emergency and temporary accommodation for supporters, directing them to improvised campsites, gymnasia with camp beds, and so on.

It should be noted that the official tourist offices in certain cities work only usual office hours during the tournament and are therefore closed and inaccessible in the evenings and sometimes on a Sunday or a public holiday, which are nonetheless match days when large numbers of foreign supporters arrive in town. This kind of structural malfunctioning is offset by the flexible way in which fan embassies operate and the availability of their staff.

In an ideal world, it is more effective for the fan embassy to operate as a separate entity, but one in permanent contact with the tourist office, which should be playing its role in centralising hotel reservations and offering advice about conventional accommodation. It is not a good thing for fan embassies to be overloaded with this kind of accommodation-related work, for they should mainly be looking for alternative solutions or providing responses when emergency situations arise. Nevertheless, the fan embassy team may be supplemented with staff from the tourist department, or even be located inside the tourist office with positive results.

*Travel*

Moving around the country, within its cities and to and from its football grounds, is a major challenge during tournaments, and the quality of information provided on the subject is particularly important. Not only city maps, but also public transport timetables (for trains, buses, trams and underground railways) should be available, and supporters should be provided with information corresponding to their personal needs. Information similarly needs to be provided about public and privately owned parking areas in the city or near the ground, park-and-ride facilities and the timetables of shuttles to the ground (ideally with a stop at the fan embassy).

*Theft or loss of documents*

Official documents, such as identity cards, passports and social security documents, as well as airline tickets, among other things, are very frequently lost or stolen during tournaments, often causing much dismay to the supporter who feels lost in an unknown environment and has to try to cope with a foreign language. Supporters need the benefit of a direct link or of having their problems dealt with directly by the fan embassy, the reception facilities and hospitality of which come into their own when this kind of problem has to be solved. In this context the presence of a diplomat from the official embassy is vital, and plays a major role, as experience has shown. It should be noted that the presence of a member of the police prevention service (clearly identified as not having a law enforcement or supervisory role) proves a considerable bonus.

*Health care*

Fan embassies need to be able to supply information about hospitals, ordinary or emergency medical services, emergency dentists and social security systems, so that supporters can be pointed in the right direction.

*Activities*

Fan embassies are the central sources of information about leisure, sports and cultural activities organised for local people, or specifically for supporters, in the city or in other parts of the country, as well as details of how to get there. Such activities are sometimes even organised at fan embassies themselves, by or for supporters, and these extend to concerts, games and other activities.

It is vital that information should be up to date, and that the very latest news should be passed on, for many activities are organised too late to be publicised in official literature, or, alternative activities may not be included in this. Other activities, news of which should be circulated mainly by the fan embassy, include public screenings of matches, which are not always planned in advance and sometimes provide a last-minute solution to the problem of channelling the movements of spectators who cannot be accommodated at a sold-out match.

*Embassies in transit cities*

As well as setting up the basic fan embassies in host cities, additional facilities can usefully be set up in those cities through which large numbers of fans will pass, or where large numbers will be staying. Such cities are those which have tourist attractions, are centres of entertainment, offer attractive activities or have large numbers of hotel rooms likely to be used by many supporters, or cities located in such a geographical position that supporters will inevitably pass through.

These scaled-down facilities can easily be placed within ordinary official services, such as tourist offices. One of their roles is also to provide information about the tournament's host cities.

*Embassies for local fans*

It is useful to set up an information centre for local fans at the ground, so that they can obtain information and so that first-line preventive work can be done, but a classic fan embassy in the city with large numbers of staff is not justified over the whole period of the tournament.

*Finance*

If it is to operate effectively, a fan embassy will incur significant logistical and staff costs. In view of the one-off nature of the event, part of the needs may be met with equipment, premises and staff made available by local authorities and associations. However, special funding is essential. Governments and tournament organisers must play their part in providing the necessary funding and support for the facility.

## Accompanying persons

Fans are a heterogeneous group which is constantly on the move. Prevention workers must therefore be out in the field, able to move flexibly and to provide an active link between the various groups of fans and the fixed structures. It also has to be borne in mind that large numbers of fans travel independently and do not take advantage of officially organised journeys. It is therefore necessary throughout the tournament to provide official staff to accompany these supporters, comprising persons from the fans' countries of origin, speaking the language and perfectly familiar with the culture of the national supporters.

In this context, the accompanying persons play an important role, as they move around with the supporters wherever they go, both in the city and at the ground. They thus play a roving fan ambassador role. As the other security services and all who are involved in the prevention effort, they are also responsible for guiding supporters to their fan embassies. These "fan ambassadors" moreover help to develop and strengthen a positive fan culture focusing on respect and tolerance.

*Role and tasks*

Quality is central to the work, in view of the lack of proportion between the large numbers of supporters and the necessarily small number of accompanying persons. The accompanying persons travel with their national supporters wherever they go within the host country, basing their movements on the dates of the fixtures. They are present in the host city on the day before, the day of and the day after the game. They also travel to other places if large numbers of fans are present there.

Their main duty is to look after the visiting supporters and to provide appropriate services so as to improve the reception given to supporters and optimise the hospitality shown to them. They provide the fans with information and help them to solve problems, in close consultation with the fan embassy and the national support unit. They also mediate between police and supporters, facilitating dialogue between them. They defuse tension and settle disputes, in order to avoid police intervention. They act as a roving unit, not only in the city and at matches, but also throughout the host nation. They work largely in urban areas, for it is the stewards who are responsible at the football grounds themselves. Nevertheless, within each ground, the accompanying persons may provide useful help to the stewards in terms of both the translation of languages and "cultural translation".

The information communicated by accompanying persons to local authorities relates to facts that may influence the course of events or the general atmosphere, or even the state of mind of a specific group. This information should always be of a general nature and should be passed on with a view to preventing major incidents. It cannot be individual, and accompanying persons must never act as police informers or "spotters". Were the roles to be blurred, negative consequences might ensue which it would be difficult to remedy, and these could short-circuit the preventive arrangements in their entirety.

*Structure*

A seven-strong team of accompanying persons for each foreign country can operate throughout the tournament. Each team should have a leader who liaises directly with the local authorities and acts as her or his group's main contact.

Team leaders work in direct liaison with a "pilot" (or "guide") from the host country, who liaises with the national support unit and ensures that information is disseminated efficiently both horizontally and vertically.

*Recruitment, selection and training*

The host country's public body in charge of prevention at the tournament can be responsible for recruitment, on the basis of names put forward by the federations, supporters' associations or official institutions of the visiting country. The selection criteria applied are independence, adaptability, communication skills and an outgoing nature. A fundamental requirement is that such staff should endorse the philosophy of the prevention programme, which is part of an official activity and must not work against institutions.

It is helpful if an attempt is also made during recruitment to target persons from visiting countries' local population (immigrants). It is a fact that certain countries, such as Turkey and Italy, are supported largely by fans that live in the organising country or neighbouring states. Other nations also have a considerable number of immigrant fans on the spot, among them Spain, Italy and Portugal.

In view of the specific nature of international tournaments and the methodological and cultural diversity of the duties of accompanying persons, depending on the country concerned, it is a good idea that full training should be provided in the weeks before the tournament begins, covering the following aspects:

- theoretical: the general organisation of the tournament, the role and duties of accompanying persons, policing arrangements, legislation, channels of communication;
- practical: visits to cities and grounds, information about logistical arrangements, meeting local authorities, police, associations and all involved in prevention;
- practice: practical experience and test on the occasion of an international match, working with the organiser's security arrangements and the police.

The desired profile for accompanying persons does not necessarily have to be that of someone who does the work professionally or of someone who works in the education sphere with hooligans or with juvenile delinquents. As their tasks are mainly those of primary prevention aimed at all supporters, it may be beneficial not to be led by professional reflexes or different work practices.

It would be useful if in-service training at international level could be provided, so as to increase the professionalism of this activity, give it overall consistency and thereby ensure that the specialised teams of "accompanying persons" perform effectively and keep pace with the constant developments that occur.

*National and international co-ordination*

A national prevention support unit makes it possible to ensure that the project as a whole is consistent and to provide general supervision. It has to ensure that activities and facilities at local level are relevant and are harmonised in the context of the general prevention policy. It provides logistical support to local teams and helps to solve problems relating to travel, accommodation, communications, etc. The support unit also co-ordinates and centralises all the information collected in the field from fan embassies, accompanying persons and prevention "pilots" or co-ordinators.

The quality of event management can be improved, the arrangements made coherent and acquired experience turned to advantage if an international body of accompanying persons is available to carry out preventive duties during international tournaments such as the World Cup and the European championships, backing up local facilities. These arrangements can even be extended to inter-club matches during Union of European Football Associations (UEFA) cup competitions.

It would be useful to set up an "international contact point" to co-ordinate the facilities and to facilitate the centralisation of information, but at the same time disseminating this information to national contact points.

**Relations between clubs and supporters**

*Supporters' charter*

When club and supporters enter into a partnership, the rights and duties of each partner have to be taken into account. This process takes place in a series of stages, starting with the making of contact and continuing with dialogue and exchanges of ideas, the taking into account by each of the needs and expectations of the other and, inevitably, the formalisation of the move so as to ensure that it will endure and that each partner has a permanent point of reference. In an ideal world, this formalisation involves a joint charter drawn up by the club and the representatives of its supporters' associations, setting out the club's obligations to its supporters and the supporters' obligations towards the club and clearly defining each party's rights and duties.

There are many examples of this, including the English Football Federation's "consumer charter" and, at a more local level, the initiative taken in Barcelona, where the supporters' charter is just one of a wider range of prevention activities based on communication and partnership with local authorities, clubs and the media, centring on the value of fair play in sport. The introduction of a "European Charter" could serve as a basis for national and local charters.

*Club officials responsible for supporter relations and associations of fans*

Clubs must value official supporters' associations, encourage their setting up and allot them a role in the context of club management. Opportunities for communication and consultation organised within the club, in the form of three-monthly "round table" sessions, should make dialogue and exchanges possible, with each party having a feeling of involvement. Supporters must be given a role in the life of the club in the broad sense, as well as in particular aspects thereof. Sports organisations can, by giving a consultative role to supporters in relation to club policy and certain decisions, especially where sporting and investment issues are concerned, as well as security management, enable their supporters to shoulder greater responsibility.

Taking as an example the role of club security managers, a member of management (that is a club official with decision-making authority) should be made responsible for relations with fans, so as to ensure that supporters' associations receive support and that the process of communication between club and fans is a concrete and permanent one.

Several European clubs have taken the lead and tried out this kind of step, with genuine success. Examples are *Standard Liège* and a fair number of German clubs.

*Supporters' departments*

If there is to be a two-way process in the management of relations with supporters, a fixed and permanent structure needs to be set up entirely devoted to this aspect. "Supporters' departments" are units which are organisationally part of the club, based within the club's infrastructure and employing supporters on the basis of work contracts. Their task is to manage all aspects of the club's relations with supporters: ticketing, fixture list, information, organisation of travel to matches and regulations.

A supporters' department is a special interface between the club and its supporters. It is an internal unit, but one open to the surrounding environment, offering permanent two-way traffic between supporters and club management. The French club *Paris St Germain* (PSG), provides a good example of this practice.

**The club's role in its social environment**

*Working with the community*

By preparing young players and managing youth teams, football clubs play an important role in educating young people and in emphasising the value of sporting ethics.

Over and above this, clubs must be in step with their environment and must open up to the life of society as a whole.

Football is a social phenomenon and a part of society. Its link with society must not be limited to match days, or stop where the sporting competition ends.

As clubs have a high symbolic value, they should play a leading role within their neighbourhood, their community and the whole of their environment throughout the week. The club can play a pivotal role in supporting broader social policies and can represent a genuine driving force for the promotion of sport and for encouraging the learning process for young people, and even for supporting good citizenship.

There are various noteworthy examples which show the way and deserve methodical and structured adoption elsewhere.

One is the community programmes run in England. One of many examples of these is at Leeds United, which has a partnership with the Ministry of Education under which it organises remedial lessons for children who have difficulties at school, with classes being held by official teachers at the ground, to which pupils are brought in vehicles bearing the club's logo. Maximum voluntary participation has been achieved, as has a clear improvement in the children's results.

Another example is that of the *Lille Métropole* (LOSC), in Lille, which has set up a "social unit" to promote the playing of football in residential neighbourhoods, to organise amateur football tournaments and to involve professional players in campaigns which highlight the value of sporting activities and sports ethics.

Some clubs in the Czech Republic, with the help of government programmes, have set up junior fan clubs, aimed at very young supporters (from 8 to 12 years), and these run sporting and educational activities, as well as offering social assistance with the help of a social worker, at a clubhouse which is a centre for leisure activities. The aim is to highlight such groups of young supporters with a positive mentality and positive behaviour, thereby giving rise to a "new" culture of sport and developing a new generation of fans who will remain loyal.

The numerous local initiatives deserve support and an international framework. It would be useful in this context to appoint within every national federation, and at UEFA and the Fédération Internationale de Football Association (FIFA), a person to be responsible for "prevention and social programmes", who would co-ordinate activities and provide institutional support for them.

*The city at the stadium and the stadium in the city*

The spectators who attend sports events are ordinary people going about their everyday lives. The football ground is the place where these different kinds of people come together, and sport provides a potential link between all the various component parts of the urban community, encouraging positive group action centring on the sporting event. In the context of a sport policy run hand in hand with a policy for the city, the football ground may provide a vital link in the chain of urban management.

The football ground should play a full part in the life of the city, so that the people who live in the city also belong at the football ground. An illustration of this comes from St Denis, where the World Cup and the new national stadium were used in the effort to foster the involvement of Parisians in the sporting sphere and to fit the sporting infrastructure into its role as part of the city. Firstly by taking advantage of the pool of jobs to which the World Cup gave rise, in synergy with the social reintegration programmes being run with young people in the neighbourhoods, secondly by organising tours of the stadium for local people to show that it remained accessible, and finally by organising multicultural days in the context of the sporting event, in the form of a "carnivalcade" in which all local associations and authorities took part.

**The role of local authorities**

*Educational activities*

Local authorities should co-ordinate and support activities that use sport as a tool for prevention or reintegration, especially activities run in schools or targeting school pupils. In Austria, for example, some activities are organised to teach school pupils about fair play and tolerance, and to inculcate in them respect for other cultures, by making them aware of the need to combat racism. At the same time, the Football against Racism in Europe network (FARE) runs national and international campaigns against racism.

In the urban context, one of the main focal points for action is that of disadvantaged areas (sink estates), to which priority is given where policies of prevention through sport are concerned. It is vital to provide facilities to enable young people from disadvantaged communities to engage in sport on a regular basis and in a structured context, and for financial considerations not to constitute an obstacle to this.

As for amateur sport, it must not be neglected. It is the basis of all sporting activity. While the media focus first and foremost on professional sport, the problems of violence are also significant in day-to-day sport, especially in amateur football.

The "school football league" project in Ostrava (Czech Republic) targets children aged 12 and 13, offering them a championship accompanied by social events, while a campaign continues to raise awareness of the fair play dimension of football, and, at the same time, the "amateur" dimension of sport is promoted.

In addition to awareness-raising campaigns, targeted action is needed among amateur clubs and those who take part in sport. There is a need for effective co-ordination of this activity at local level.

We shall cite as an example a French scheme involving legislation which provides for an "officer responsible for the prevention of violence in sport" to be appointed in twenty-three departments, this officer acting as a resource person and a facilitator for local sporting associations, institutions and other bodies, with a view to combating violence in amateur sport.

*The need for a "contractual commitment": the role of advisory committees for the prevention of violence in sport*

Under the aegis of the local authority, a committee made up of members who play an active part in fan coaching, the police, the football club and the courts, in combination with youth and sports associations and the university, can co-ordinate the activities carried out and give thought on a permanent basis to the problem of violence in sport. The committee is also responsible for offering opinions and sending proposals to the local authority relating to the shape to be given to prevention policy and to the specific programmes needed to meet the requirements.

This standing committee provides an opportunity for the partners to consult each other, exchange opinions and discuss matters with a view to making the action taken on the ground as effective as possible. In view of its institutional position, it also acts as a direct intermediary between those who work in the field and policy-makers. Another of its functions is to give impetus to specific projects involving the partners, either in the form of awareness-raising campaigns or through highly targeted action meeting effective needs.

As those involved have a privileged position because of their involvement in the field, this committee may act as a "local observatory of violence in sport" and detect any new tendencies, while guaranteeing a credible and co-ordinated assessment of the problem, with a view to speedy, appropriate and effective responses.

*Activities for local people during international tournaments*

Related activities need to be held to raise awareness among local people and encourage them to get involved in the event, so that the festive dimension of the tournament and the concept of hospitality come right to the fore. If this is done, a convivial atmosphere will bind everyone together in the spirit of fraternity everyone expects during the tournament.

The tournament, with all its heavy symbolism, should act as a catalyst for larger-scale preventive activities. The dissemination of the values of tolerance and respect is encouraged through multicultural activities and awareness-raising campaigns.

*Awareness-raising campaigns*

Awareness must be raised among local people through preventive campaigns. One example of a very worthwhile initiative is that of the primary prevention activities undertaken in the "Welkom!" schools project in the Netherlands.

It is necessary to emphasise the festive side of the event, as well as the concept of fair play, and, quite particularly, to demystify the mood of panic inevitably generated by the media in the preparatory phase of such tournaments. Tension in the local population must be reduced, and people prepared for a fraternal festival of football, rather than for confrontations with foreign invaders with a thirst for both beer and violence.

Another aim is to create an atmosphere conducive to relaxation and leisure, as was achieved in Bordeaux when Scotland played there in 1998, and in Liège, where Norway played in 2000, so as to avoid cities being left deserted, as occurred in Toulouse during the 1998 World Cup.

People who run pubs and bars are a specific target, for they play a vital part in preventing over-consumption of alcohol. Both staff and management of alcohol outlets need to be made aware of their responsibilities. Information needs to be targeted at them so as to reduce the likelihood of incidents occurring.

*Targeted prevention*

An effort must be made to avoid making an already socially vulnerable group of the population feel excluded. The tournament and all that goes with it must not be the preserve of a few privileged people. Preventive activities need to be carried out in local estates, especially those considered difficult.

Such activities should take further local policies on integration through sport and on intercultural prevention, and should be organised in co-operation with associations and similar bodies that have experience of socio-preventive work. Alternative activities can be organised to avoid leaving people at a loose end or bored, a situation which often leads to offences being committed, examples of such activities being sporting tournaments, "taster" sessions in certain sports, themed evenings, concerts and educational activities. Such activities also have a structuring function if they are part of a carefully considered educational project. And they distract the attention of young people from their potential interest in possible conflict areas and from participation in clashes.

## Conclusion

It has become vital for Europe to adopt a common approach to the prevention of violence at football grounds. A common and concerted international preventive response is needed, as hooliganism becomes international and the various countries experience similar problems. This means that local, national and international structures are required.

The various proposals for action made in this study are based on experiments in progress, which have shown some degree of effectiveness, or on existing needs that require an appropriate response. These initiatives open up a range of solutions for developing integrated preventive activities of a high standard, suited to local needs.

The various European countries are showing a genuine will to combat violence in sport through preventive strategies, and they are taking effective action at local and national level, showing great creativity, and underpinned by great professionalism. It also has to be said that there is a certain amount of local or national partitioning, making it necessary to ensure that prevention practice details are exchanged internationally and disseminated. The aim being to ensure that good practice is promoted and is able to be applied elsewhere. At the same time, and in more concrete terms, the appointment by each country of a national contact person, within an official institutional structure responsible for centralising information about prevention in the football sphere and for disseminating this information, will make possible better communication in support of operational efforts, as well as a certain "standardisation" of approaches.

The interlinking of these contact persons (or "national correspondents") necessitates international co-ordination within an official structure acting as a relay between the "national correspondents", and also maintaining permanent contact with the relevant international institutions and international sports federations.

Prevention is improving gradually, but constantly. As it develops further, it will help to improve qualitatively the management of spectator violence and to provide structural support for the management of major sports events.

## BIBLIOGRAPHY

*Spectator behaviour, media coverage and crowd control at the 1998 European football championships*, 1990: Council of Europe

"Direct visiting in social work with the juvenile football fan scene. A general concept for the nationwide establishment of fan projects" (ref. T-RV (92) 11), 1992: Council of Europe

"Report of the Secretary General" (ref. MSL-9 (2000)) 10 Rev.) and "Adopted Texts" (MSL-9 (2000) 11), 9th Conference of European Ministers responsible for Sport, Bratislava, 30-31 May 2000: Council of Europe

"Evaluation of Euro 2000" (Belgium) (ref. T-RV (2001) 5) and "Evaluation of Euro 2000: hospitality" (Netherlands) (ref. T-RV (2001) 6), meeting, Strasbourg 31 January, 2001: Council of Europe

"National reports" (ref. T-RV (2001) 13) and "Meeting report" (ref. T-RV (2001)16), 21st meeting of the Standing Committee of the European Convention on Spectator Violence, Strasbourg, 20-21 June 2001: Council of Europe

"Prevention of violence at major sports events: compilation of reports" (ref. T-RV (2001) 19), European Convention on Spectator Violence: Council of Europe

"Euro 2000: review of the prevention measures", Permanent Secretariat for Prevention Policy, Ministry of the Interior, Brussels, 2001 (booklet edited by the Ministry of Interior – Permanent Secretariat for the Prevention Policy – Brussels).

# Sales agents for publications of the Council of Europe
# Agents de vente des publications du Conseil de l'Europe

**AUSTRALIA/AUSTRALIE**
Hunter Publications, 58A, Gipps Street
AUS-3066 COLLINGWOOD, Victoria
Tel.: (61) 3 9417 5361
Fax: (61) 3 9419 7154
E-mail: Sales@hunter-pubs.com.au
http://www.hunter-pubs.com.au

**BELGIUM/BELGIQUE**
La Librairie européenne SA
50, avenue A. Jonnart
B-1200 BRUXELLES 20
Tel.: (32) 2 734 0281
Fax: (32) 2 735 0860
E-mail: info@libeurop.be
http://www.libeurop.be

Jean de Lannoy
202, avenue du Roi
B-1190 BRUXELLES
Tel.: (32) 2 538 4308
Fax: (32) 2 538 0841
E-mail: jean.de.lannoy@euronet.be
http://www.jean-de-lannoy.be

**CANADA**
Renouf Publishing Company Limited
5369 Chemin Canotek Road
CDN-OTTAWA, Ontario, K1J 9J3
Tel.: (1) 613 745 2665
Fax: (1) 613 745 7660
E-mail: order.dept@renoufbooks.com
http://www.renoufbooks.com

**CZECH REPUBLIC/
RÉPUBLIQUE TCHÈQUE**
Suweco Cz Dovoz Tisku Praha
Ceskomoravska 21
CZ-18021 PRAHA 9
Tel.: (420) 2 660 35 364
Fax: (420) 2 683 30 42
E-mail: import@suweco.cz

**DENMARK/DANEMARK**
GAD Direct
Fiolstaede 31-33
DK-1171 COPENHAGEN K
Tel.: (45) 33 13 72 33
Fax: (45) 33 12 54 94
E-mail: info@gaddirect.dk

**FINLAND/FINLANDE**
Akateeminen Kirjakauppa
Keskuskatu 1, PO Box 218
FIN-00381 HELSINKI
Tel.: (358) 9 121 41
Fax: (358) 9 121 4450
E-mail: akatilaus@stockmann.fi
http://www.akatilaus.akateeminen.com

**FRANCE**
La Documentation française
(Diffusion/Vente France entière)
124, rue H. Barbusse
F-93308 AUBERVILLIERS Cedex
Tel.: (33) 01 40 15 70 00
Fax: (33) 01 40 15 68 00
E-mail: commandes.vel@ladocfrancaise.gouv.fr
http://www.ladocfrancaise.gouv.fr

Librairie Kléber (Vente Strasbourg)
Palais de l'Europe
F-67075 STRASBOURG Cedex
Fax: (33) 03 88 52 91 21
E-mail: librairie.kleber@coe.int

**GERMANY/ALLEMAGNE
AUSTRIA/AUTRICHE**
UNO Verlag
Am Hofgarten 10
D-53113 BONN
Tel.: (49) 2 28 94 90 20
Fax: (49) 2 28 94 90 222
E-mail: bestellung@uno-verlag.de
http://www.uno-verlag.de

**GREECE/GRÈCE**
Librairie Kauffmann
28, rue Stadiou
GR-ATHINAI 10564
Tel.: (30) 1 32 22 160
Fax: (30) 1 32 30 320
E-mail: ord@otenet.gr

**HUNGARY/HONGRIE**
Euro Info Service
Hungexpo Europa Kozpont ter 1
H-1101 BUDAPEST
Tel.: (361) 264 8270
Fax: (361) 264 8271
E-mail: euroinfo@euroinfo.hu
http://www.euroinfo.hu

**ITALY/ITALIE**
Libreria Commissionaria Sansoni
Via Duca di Calabria 1/1, CP 552
I-50125 FIRENZE
Tel.: (39) 556 4831
Fax: (39) 556 41257
E-mail: licosa@licosa.com
http://www.licosa.com

**NETHERLANDS/PAYS-BAS**
De Lindeboom Internationale Publikaties
PO Box 202, MA de Ruyterstraat 20 A
NL-7480 AE HAAKSBERGEN
Tel.: (31) 53 574 0004
Fax: (31) 53 572 9296
E-mail: lindeboo@worldonline.nl
http://home-1-worldonline.nl/~lindeboo/

**NORWAY/NORVÈGE**
Akademika, A/S Universitetsbokhandel
PO Box 84, Blindern
N-0314 OSLO
Tel.: (47) 22 85 30 30
Fax: (47) 23 12 24 20

**POLAND/POLOGNE**
Główna Ksiegarnia Naukowa
im. B. Prusa
Krakowskie Przedmiescie 7
PL-00-068 WARSZAWA
Tel.: (48) 29 22 66
Fax: (48) 22 26 64 49
E-mail: inter@internews.com.pl
http://www.internews.com.pl

**PORTUGAL**
Livraria Portugal
Rua do Carmo, 70
P-1200 LISBOA
Tel.: (351) 13 47 49 82
Fax: (351) 13 47 02 64
E-mail: liv.portugal@mail.telepac.pt

**SPAIN/ESPAGNE**
Mundi-Prensa Libros SA
Castelló 37
E-28001 MADRID
Tel.: (34) 914 36 37 00
Fax: (34) 915 75 39 98
E-mail: libreria@mundiprensa.es
http://www.mundiprensa.com

**SWITZERLAND/SUISSE**
BERSY
Route de Monteiller
CH-1965 SAVIESE
Tel.: (41) 27 395 53 33
Fax: (41) 27 395 53 34
E-mail: jprausis@netplus.ch

Adeco – Van Diermen
Chemin du Lacuez 41
CH-1807 BLONAY
Tel.: (41) 21 943 26 73
Fax: (41) 21 943 36 05
E-mail: info@adeco.org

**UNITED KINGDOM/ROYAUME-UNI**
TSO (formerly HMSO)
51 Nine Elms Lane
GB-LONDON SW8 5DR
Tel.: (44) 207 873 8372
Fax: (44) 207 873 8200
E-mail: customer.services@theso.co.uk
http://www.the-stationery-office.co.uk
http://www.itsofficial.net

**UNITED STATES and CANADA/
ÉTATS-UNIS et CANADA**
Manhattan Publishing Company
468 Albany Post Road, PO Box 850
CROTON-ON-HUDSON,
NY 10520, USA
Tel.: (1) 914 271 5194
Fax: (1) 914 271 5856
E-mail: Info@manhattanpublishing.com
http://www.manhattanpublishing.com

---

Council of Europe Publishing/Editions du Conseil de l'Europe
F-67075 Strasbourg Cedex
Tel.: (33) 03 88 41 25 81 – Fax: (33) 03 88 41 39 10 – E-mail: publishing@coe.int – Website: http://book.coe.int